T0319189

Shadow and Dream
Alive in Poetry

Harry O. Garuba

Langaa Research & Publishing CIG
Mankon, Bamenda

Publisher
Langaa RPCIG
Langaa Research & Publishing Common Initiative Group
P.O. Box 902 Mankon
Bamenda
North West Region
Cameroon
Langaagrp@gmail.com
www.langaa-rpcig.net

Distributed in and outside N. America by African Books Collective
orders@africanbookscollective.com
www.africanbookscollective.com

ISBN-10: 9956-553-87-5

ISBN-13: 978-9956-553-87-7

© Harry O. Garuba 2023

First published as *Shadow and Dream: And Other Poems* in 1982
(New Horn Press, Ibadan, Nigeria)

Harry O. Garuba

The Realisation of a Creative Dream

Harry Oludare Garuba was born at Akure in 1958. He lived as a boy in various towns in the West and Midwest of Nigeria before proceeding in 1968 to Government College, Ughelli, for his secondary education. From there he moved to Edo College, Benin City, for his Higher School Certificate course. After a brief spell in television, he entered the University of Ibadan where he took a Bachelor's degree in English in 1978 and a Master's degree in the same discipline in 1980.

Professor Garuba passed away in February 2020. He was a towering poet, essayist, literary scholar and public intellectual with an impressive record of social responsiveness in scholarship. First, in Nigeria where he was born, studied, practiced journalism and started his career as a university lecturer. Second, in South Africa, where he moved in 1998, assumed positions at the universities of Zululand and Cape Town, served with single-minded dedication, loyalty, humility and commitment to transformation and decolonization beyond lip service and beyond essentialism. He was adored by his students, as evidenced in the outpouring of heartfelt tributes at his funeral and memorial services organized in his honour, as well as in obituaries published in newspapers in South Africa, Nigeria and beyond. Many of his students and colleagues in the academy are currently working on various edited volumes of essays and tributes in his honour, a testament to the popularity and esteem he enjoyed as a scholar, a mentor and a luminary.

Not only was Professor Garuba an accomplished academic and public intellectual, he was also a model father and citizen of Nigeria and South Africa who preached by example how to foster conviviality and Pan-Africanism by building bridges and discouraging the zero sum games of power and privilege that plague the contemporary world. This, he exemplified in his scholarship as well. One of the projects he was working on before his passing, was a bilateral research project jointly funded by the South African National Research Foundation (NRF) and the Japanese Society for the Promotion of Science (JSPS), titled "Citizenship in Motion: South African and Japanese scholars in conversation." His contribution to the book discussing the research results in the network was an essay titled: "Spectres of Citizenship: Reflections on the Hauntologies of Belonging in Zakes Mda's *Ways of Dying*."

Let me share a paragraph from the essay that speaks to the depth, breadth and interdisciplinary nature and currency of Professor Garuba's scholarship, and to why I and many others found him a colleague of outstanding distinction to work with – someone truly worthy of recognition and celebration in his lifetime and posthumously, a giant on whose shoulders future generations would stand to excel. Garuba writes:

> This chapter focuses on an actual practice of citizenship, as represented in a work of narrative fiction, that carries all these traces and scars of a past that is not past. It explores the spectres that haunt the normative notion of citizenship in contemporary South Africa. Beyond South Africa, it must be said, the spectre of citizenship haunts the contemporary world. First articulated as a claim to a specific form of belonging that creates horizontal affiliation among people/populations, citizenship also rapidly – simultaneously, some may argue – became an instrument for legitimising exclusions, of determining who counts, who matters, on the one hand, and who is dis-counted and who is considered disposable, on the other. In the colonial world, disposability was not simply notional; it was one of the major technologies of rule. Citizenship acquired significance because it specified an order of belonging, a regime of rights and obligations, anchored on a political rationality framed around the priority of the rational subject, the nation and of democracy. However, as indicated earlier, citizenship was also defined in opposition to its Other/s, or, as Chatterjee states it, by its 'exceptions.'
>
> The spectral Other/s in the shadow of citizenship has lately become more visible in the age of Donald Trump, the rise of the nationalist far right, xenophobia and the televised plight of refugees across the world, particularly from Myanmar and the Mediterranean to the US–Mexico border. In short, it has become quite clear that the intelligibility of the notion of citizenship depends on its exclusions, its spectral

others, from the slave to the refugee. The more visible presence of the slave (cf: Nima Elbagir's CNN documentary of *Slave Auctions in Libya*) and the refugee on the horizon of our vision shows that what haunts citizenship is not only its violent excretions (in form of those it expels) and the spectre of social death but death in the physical, literal sense, pure and simple. The images of dead babies, of bodies picked up from the sea have migrated from the confines of detention centres and the documents of immigration NGOs into our living rooms. In spite of the deaths that lurk everywhere, the quest for citizenship is still largely propelled forward by displacing and repressing this understanding of its hauntology of death and ghostly presences and focusing on its narrative of benefits, belonging and affiliation. But what happens when this narrative is pressed to its limits? What happens when the struggle for this ideal of citizenship falls apart at the moment of its attainment? The moment when the quest produces its own requiem such as is represented in these stories of those excluded at its borders and – for our purposes – as depicted in the first pages of Zakes Mda's (1995) novel *Ways of Dying*? (Garuba 2019: 385-386)

Whether in poetry or in scholarly essays, the dreams and plight of those in the shadows of citizenship and social visibility were a permanent concern of Harry's.

In resonance with Garuba's pan-African commitments and investment in social responsiveness, it is noteworthy that one of his very last international scholarly activities was a visit to Ghana in August 2019 to promote the book on citizenship, and speak to his chapter in a series of seminars at the University of Education in Winneba and the University of Ghana in Accra. The cover photo of this collection was taken in Winneba, about an hour before Harry's seminar presentation.

Thirty five years after the publication of his first collection of poetry, *Shadow and Dream and Other Poems*, his second volume, *Animist Chants and Memorials: Poems* was released. With both works, Garuba's creative and intellectual life had come full circle. The first collection signalled a talented poet's awakening. The second book announced the attainment of full artistic maturity. But in between, Garuba was busy exploring multiple African identities within the context of often problematic modernities and hence his groundbreaking studies on the phenomenon of animism as a fundamental postcolonial condition. He was always painstaking in both his creative and intellectual pursuits and the re-issue of his first book of poetry revisits the question of his diligence which stems from a deeply humanist understanding of the quest for perfection which is of course not also without fundamental flaws. It is my hope that bringing back into circulation Garuba's first collection of poetry will enchant youths and elders to embrace and celebrate his genius and inspirational humanism.

Francis B. Nyamnjoh
University of Cape Town

Reference

Garuba, H. (2019) "Spectres of Citizenship: Reflections on the Hauntologies of Belonging in Zakes Mda's *Ways of Dying*", in: Itsuhiro Hazama, Kiyoshi Umeya, Francis B. Nyamnjoh (eds), *Citizenship in Motion: South African and Japanese Scholars in Conversation*, Bamenda: Langaa, pp.383-399.

Table of Contents

Four Folk Figures

Harry Garuba:
A Priest at Christopher Okigbo's Shrine

Harry Garuba arrived on the Nigerian poetry circuit as a fully formed poet even though he was a young man in his early twenties. He was immediately received as not only a prince of poets but also a man of the people on account of his untiring gregariousness, effortless charm and almost heartbreaking tenderness. Harry adored beauty, and most especially, poetic beauty. He was born a poet. He didn't even have to write poetry. Remarkably, he managed to fill the seemingly barren moments of his life with poetry and its varied cadences. His looks, smile and composure radiated poetry and the intimacy of gentle and perpetual communion. He embarked on a quest by standing still but his stillness was not informed by stasis or regression. Instead, it seemed to be buoyed by the energetic movement of deep waters beneath the surface of a river. Harry's apparently simple poetry masked easily overlooked layers of meaning, pathos and ellipsis.

The flow of his poetry mirrored the natural patterns of his speech and the manner in which his soul moved and revealed itself as calibrated sequences of creative grace. He was exceptionally courageous in offering up his inner truths and vulnerabilities. He broke down hardened defences with his generosity and naiveté. Indeed, his poetry was an integral part of his carefully moulded world, and his world was nurtured through a warm, fuzzy glow that was similar to the air that gave luxuriant leaves even more colour, density and radiance.

Harry did not find his voice totally independent of illustrious forebears. He was an acolyte of the great Christopher Okigbo. He never grew weary of reciting lines from the visionary poet's oeuvre or finding new ways by which to celebrate and immortalise him. Okigbo was the undisputed patron-saint of the University of Ibadan (UI), Nigeria, based poets where Harry had studied and worked. They sang and rhapsodised at Okigbo's altar, they drank wine at his fount and inhaled the mists that emanated from the face of the immortal poet's moon. Indeed, Okigbo was akin to a deity whose name was not mentioned recklessly or in vain. Harry never baulked at teaching his own significant gathering of admirers how to honour and revere Okigbo. He was first and foremost a high priest in the hallowed shrine of the inestimable poet.

Along with a few friends, Harry established the Poetry Club at UI Ibadan in the early 1980s and Okigbo Night was the highlight of the academic calendar in which poetry competitions, readings and reflections were held to commemorate the slain poet who was killed during the Nigerian Civil War in 1967.

Indeed, Okigbo was not only a poet's poet but also an incorrigible man of action. And so, nothing could prevent him from playing a role-which turned out to be fatal- in the horrendous war. Okigbo's unchallenged lyricism is expansive, celestial and borderless. In his unique existential trajectory, the supreme lyrical poet embraced unequivocally, the fate of a star-crossed man of war with utterly devastating consequences.

Harry, on the other hand, committed to the art of lyricism and the unalloyed purity of the supreme poetic vision. Indeed, he was a lyrical poet blessed with a lyrical spirit and the thought of wreaking unwarranted violence upon anyone or anything was difficult for him to conceive. The realm of politics was also not meant for him as an active participant. He preferred to eschew the cloak and dagger realities of politics and chose to pursue Okigbo's original idea of aestheticism to its ultimate resolution which was to locate, isolate and refine the essence of poetic beauty *in extremis*.

Such a radical conception of the art of poetry was cultivated and nurtured in the poets who converged around Harry at Ibadan. He demonstrated that in life, poetry could also be the defining philosophy of both consciousness and action. If one was not a poet and couldn't compose acceptable lines, one could, at least, will oneself into being a poet by assuming the ways and consciousness of a bard. One simply declares, "I live poetry with beauty and equanimity in my soul, thoughts and deeds. I illuminate ether with my inner light, I bless every company that encounters me with my charisma. I sing the songs that my ears have never heard but emanate directly out of you. I disregard my physical limits and confinement in order to become you". What could be greater poetry than that? This was a central credo of Harry's life.

Harry formed his uniquely tender poetic sensibility based on affect, the ethics of friendship and communion. This lyrical sensibility was evident at the very beginning and stayed with him throughout his life. It was also a sensibility much given to the beatific virtues of song, verdant nature and the unblemished human subject. Arguably, this is a vision that might have been fashioned even before he encountered Okigbo and may have been integral to whom he was as a human being.

There was also a sly element of dusky and slightly mysterious melancholia in Harry's outlook that encompassed Pablo Neruda, Cesar Vallejo, Octavio Paz, Gabriel Garcia Marquez, Mario Vargas Llosa, Manuel Puig and all the other great poetic souls (who were some of Harry's favourite authors)- even when they were ostensibly prose stylists- of South America. The grotesque sense of the macabre that convulsed and terrorised Latin America was similar to the tragic-comic visitations of gargantuan proportions that erupted frequently in Africa. If Latin America could come up with magic realism, Africa on its part, had a more original version, animist realism, with the likes of D.O. Fagunwa, Amos Tutuola, Soni Labou Tansi and Ben Okri providing us with scenarios and characters that continue to haunt us in our dreams.

Agreeing with a visiting American scholar who called Ibadan poets "tortured souls", Harry milked this ingenious moniker for all it was worth. He demonstrated that there can be a shroud of tranquillity in the manner in which distress and agony could be confronted. He showed that melancholia and unrequited love could be significant ingredients for composing timeless poetry. And when he offered a smirk in the face of life-crushing tragedy, he was only affirming the verities of immutable bitter-sweet realities. Indeed, the after-taste of sublimation bears a taint of melancholy. After a period of light and grace, there was also the inevitable descent into gloom.

Harry was a child of the Niger Delta. He understood the hidden music of their deep brown rivers and creeks. He recognised the voices of the birds that sang across dark, lush vegetation and forests. And just like the other great Nigerian poet of the delta, John Pepper Clark-Bekederemo, he understood the elemental force of nature's poetry.

Harry's *Shadow and Dream*, represents his first completely realised song about a poet's awakening at dawn. Naked in front of his baptismal waters, his reflection is pure, uncluttered and utterly inviting. He is inviting the world to drink out of the purity and generosity of his spirit, to bask in the muted illumination of unadulterated youth. He is calling on his audience to follow his reverie with the hope, courage and loyalty of first time initiates. Harry is both an initiate and a high priest tenderly making his way through frail ferns and thick grasses and the entire gamut of human emotions and consciousness to a horizon of recognition and acceptance. The fortunate denouement of this quasi-mythical-cum-poetic journey, is that, Harry, leading his band of trusting followers, reaches his destination with all the poetry of his soul and the tenderness of his vision still very much intact.

The importance of this slim collection of verse can be perceived in the totemic status it maintains amongst the so-called "third generation of Nigerian writers", most especially those engaged in poetry. In contrast to Okigbo's landmark *Labyrinths* which is an epic of grand quests both personal and collective, *Shadow and Dream* is a nuanced song of poetic efflorescence, a eulogy for youthful experience, élan and emotional adventure. But much of its subtle power stems from its measured under-statedness. Devoid of the customary braggadocio of youth, it is a guarded celebration of affect, tenderness and wholesome feelings. Ultimately, its subtlety, equanimous undertones and delicate but unfailing charm, lent a profound sense of poetic liberation to an entire generation of poets.

Sanya Osha
University of Cape Town, September, 2022

Introduction

Okigbo's Overcoat: Harry Garuba

I am Harry's student.
I can't praise him enough for what he taught me.
See the following as a modest tribute
to a great teacher by a grateful student.

The years in which the first generation of modernist poets made their appearance as leading African poets also coincided with the years in which many African countries acquired political independence after five hundred years of colonial (ist)occupation and exploitation.

Where most literary scholars attribute complexity, experimentalism, and innovation to Euromodernist poetry, the terms deployed to describe modern African poetry tend to focus on tradition, myths, authenticity, and spirituality. Such criticism of modernist African poetry fails to combine various traditions of poetry in the African context.

Tanure Ojaide's *Poetic Imagination in Black Africa* (1996) also maps the uniqueness of the African poetic imagination which is differentiated from Euromodernist aesthetics: "This authenticity manifests itself in the use of concrete images derived from the fauna and flora, proverbs, indigenous rhythms, verbal tropes, and concepts of space and time to establish a poetic form" (30).

Besides that, Harry Garuba shows the very specific characteristic of postcolonial poetry of the landscape as a challenge to the imperial eyes.

"Since colonization is first and foremost about territorial and epistemological dispossession, postcolonial poetry of the landscape and the environment also had to strive to reverse this by reclaiming cognitive and epistemological ownership of the land" (Garuba, 2017:210).

In this regard, "territorial and epistemological dispossession" determines the form of poetic understanding in post-colonial

African literature. What makes African modernist poetry significant is truly based on the poets' approach.

One of the oft-quoted sayings of the nineteenth century Russian novelist Dostoyevsky reads, "We all come out from Gogol's overcoat." This implies the tradition of writing and the lineage inside it. I think, we can easily adapt that line to African context, then, here, we shall be able to say, 'Garuba comes out of Okigbo's overcoat,' which is quite true, and admitted by Garuba himself in his latest interview as follows: "I don't think that any serious Nigerian poet writing in English can avoid the shadow of Christopher Okigbo."[1]

It is unfortunate that Garuba's poetry has not been appreciated or critiqued as much as his role in pioneering the formation of his generation. The implications and influences his poetry bears to date have yet to be studied in order to position him in the postcolonial context.

The way Garuba has captured images is not founded on observations, it is a profoundly engaged intimacy that imbricates layers of understanding the worldliness. The structure of poetry does not function to display these layers as independently constructed as well. Nigerian poet and academic Funso Aiyejina (1987) points out Garuba's concern of cultural form of society which is displaced. He reads persona as "the ear which hears the unspoken and weaves webs of dreams out of such celestial materials."

There is a strong connection between Okigbo's "Haveansgate" and Garuba's persistent intention to bring back the spiritual uprightness to poetry. Though it does not delve into mythical landscape as such, the spirituality in *Shadow and Dream* somehow shades into material vocabulary in the form of resilience.

The widely held mis/perception that the world of modernist art does not reflect the outside world, namely social reality is mainly rooted in the idea that poetic vision has no relevance to

---

[1] Ahmet Sait Akcay, *Interview with Harry Garuba on Modernist African Poetry, and his lates collection Animist Chants and Memorials*, University of Cape Town, 2019.

life which finely summed up in Oscar Wilde's bold statement, "life imitates art far more than art imitates life."

I think, this literary observation applies in a distinct way in African settings. It works through layers abovementioned until intimacy becomes mature and perfectionist. Such affection and desires for a nation as personas cherish would find their gratification in poetry which serves as a medium of selfhood.

Intimacy appears when Okigbo investigates past and present-past to construct the African setting over imperial dichotomies differentiating animistic vision and implications that sustain while in Garuba the personas feel at pains to revisit the past which is predicated on the future and saturated with anxieties.

Intimacy and anxiety become irresistible body cunningly relied on persona's dwelling. The very introverted preoccupation comes to insist for that spiritual materiality that resonates with Okigbo's calling for the river.

The persona's invocations to the nature, mainly 'dead iroko trees' which provide 'shadows' over history, work as a convergence of thought, responding to Okigbo's calling for sustained animistic values, while also anticipating many of moves of environmental approaches that led to reframe the concept of humanity crises such as post-Truth and Post-Humanist approaches.

> "... I shall
> Weave my little web of
> Dreams beneath the shadows
> Cast by these dead iroko trees."

Because the only dreams might inhabit the truth, and generate a new source outside the mainstream genealogy of time. Dreams hold facts beyond linearity of time which are survived by shadows.

These opening lines of *Shadow and Dream* echo Okigbo's calling for river Idoto, or Goddess Idoto while the persona tries to show his allegiance to Her as follows:

> "Shall I offer to Idoto
> my sandhouse and bones,
> then write no more on snow-patch?" (from "Havensgate")

Both poems are tempted to be a ritual practice of "cleansing" and their ambiance can only be captured in the light of an animistic approach. Here, Garuba's explanatory remarks on animism are helpful to account for the animistic mode of communication between objects and spirits:

> "Animism is often simply seen as belief in objects such as stones or trees or rivers for the simple reason that animist gods and spirits are located and embodied in objects: the objects are the physical and material manifestations of the gods and spirits" (Garuba, 2003:267).

By invoking 'dead iroko trees,' Garuba tries to restore the demolished African presence in history. The iroko trees are said to live up to five hundred years which also coincided with the time spanning colonialism in Africa. The following lines of "Introit" invite us to witness and more importantly to 'listen' to humming of waters.

> "I shall stand here alone
> Through this long blighted night
> I will neither sing nor
> Dance but listening to
> The murmur of the
> Ebbing waters I shall
> Weave my little web of
> Dreams beneath the shadows
> Cast by these dead iroko trees."

'Long blighted night' in the second line, referring to the longest darkness of times since the persona is alone and seeking refuge in nature, suggests that his way of knowing is now uncovered so as to transcend his observations to recognize the knowledge of truth generated through metaphors such as 'ebbing waters, 'the long blighted night' and 'the dead iroko trees'. The only way to access knowledge seems to be to give ear to non-written grammars of the universe, that of animistic mode of production.

So, the past is 'blurred' enough that held over 'the tale of elders' in the memory of persona:

> "and I recall, through frayed amber edges of a blurred past
> the memory of the strange quiet of an evening" (*Shadow and Dream*)

This is a recurrent theme that haunts poetic vision as well. Nation once glorified now embodies scattered pieces of scars, torn out and drenched in hopelessness enough. Though darkness dominates and threatens the body that potentially transforms the language into a 'slippery cobwebs,' only the extent to which we are unable to see.

> "We are all in the dark
> a dark cave from which despair threatens
> we will braid these cobwebs
> into tiny fingers of scars
> and long threads of tears
> a lacework of struggle and suffering" (To all Compatriots)

'Braiding cobwebs' and 'a lacework of struggle' here refer to a labouring which coexists with human affection and suffering as well. Once again, the past is uncovered in 'the dark cave,' which runs through tangible images. These images encourage the poet to refer to communal imagination out of labouring and suffering. Communality becomes more accessible not only through shadowy images but also the landscape on which lived experiences are truly grounded. For the political mechanism of postcolonial governance appears to be an embodiment of alienation which poet herself/himself has her/his share. When the persona says, '... dreams ruptured/in the rank screams of poli-trick-cians,' he already makes a strong case for the politicians as common tricks floating over dreams that are 'wounded' and 'ruptured.'

Garuba truly shows us the pitfalls of estrangement as a mode of production that prevails over cultural formations.

"In league
businessmen, professionals, prophets,
professors and
poets singing in the chloroform dream of money"

Then the persona cries:

"I felt
I felt
estranged. Surely the poet is
estranged who cannot share
his people's fount of being." (Estrangement: Kano'78)

As an animist poet, Garuba's poetry in many ways reflects the distinctive tendencies of the post-1980s African poetry, that is the dilemma generated by the fragmentation of nation-building. That is why, Garuba's consistent preoccupation revolves around the image of 'scar', and this image represents both the unstable agency in the postcolonies and literary intimacy.. Because the 'scars/wounds' are the most vivid and extraverted representation in literary tradition. This historical and literary engagement constructs the metaphor in order to show the human struggle and survival dating back to the ancient times.

"Dream and Shadow" is an elegy for the loss of his childhood world, of the past, of wholeness. The opening lines function to destabilize the form of unity showing dissemination of nation beside his memories of childhood which becomes unduly disruptive.

"a band of worshippers insolently intone
incantations beneath the tattered shawl of leaves
a little bird flaps its wings in the thin air
drenched in the full colour of sunset
a leaf stirs with the light wings of a meteor
and drops silently into my childhood nest of laughter"

This poem should be translated as a "fall of nation", the loss of dreams and of the past. The Persona only recalls 'a dream of wings and the horizon', for everything is falling apart. Scars are ever-present, consistently, rigorously, and pungently turning to a founding critique of structure of power which operates from the uppermost.

The main challenge comes from below, indicating the exploitation of power and culture.

> 'the egret with the beak of steel
> has descended again below skyline
> into our treasure-house of scars
> cascading down on our scar-shrines
> feigning maiden purity
> she claws at our scars,
> our only symbols of suffered ages ...' (Dream: Sea, Moon, Bird)

'The egret' here is deployed deliberately to illustrate its function through ages. For the egret is believed to be a symbol of gratitude and contentment after long suffering in Christianity. But what is concerned here is not Christian piety, it is a piety of African deities. It is a very striking image that stations the convergence that also shows how resilience and intimacy interact so as to project the parting wings of history.

Garuba converts the often-used metaphor of Christian piety to reflect on communal experience of humanity in Africa which has not been considered and appreciated in the discourse of modernity. Ramazani's term 'bricolage' functions aptly in poetic vision and shows us Garuba's strategic positioning[2] in world literatures. He reconstructs the very global metaphor in locality, namely African setting to open up a new route to engage with a wholly worldliness. It is both animistic and global.

In a nutshell, *Shadow and Dream* is a powerful critique of colonial and postcolonial registers of modernity which always

---

[2] We should also remember Garuba's reflections on African modernist poetry. Calling the first generation of West African modernist poetry "the modernist-nationalist," Garuba, in his article "The Unbearable Lightness of Being: Re-Figuring Trends in Recent Nigerian Poetry", argues: "Adopting the modernistic technique of the multi-layered narrative, these writers basically re-wrote this idiom not only introduction of what, for the moment, we may call authentically material at the level of content but also at the level of technique, they reworked it away from the disabling politics of time encoded in modernism" (Garuba, 2005:58).

come in possession of power. His contribution is to reminds us of the potential voices of the modernist African poetry and its imagination which are located as a compass to navigate the textual and historical grammars.

Ahmet Sait Akcay
University of Cape Town

Works Cited

Aiyejina, Funso. "Recent Nigerian poetry in English: A critical survey." *Kunapipi* 9.2 (1987): 5.

Garuba, Harry. "Explorations in animist materialism: Notes on reading/writing African literature, culture, and society." *Public culture* 15.2 (2003): 261-285.

Garuba, Harry. "Landscape, the Environment, and Postcolonial Poetry." *The Cambridge Companion to Postcolonial Poetry* (2017): 209-221.

Ojaide, Tanure. *Ordering the African imagination*. Malthouse press, 2007.

Ramazani, Jahan. "Modernist Bricolage, Postcolonial Hybridity." *Modernism and Colonialism* (2007): 288.

Introit

I shall stand here alone
Through this long blighted night
I will neither sing nor
Dance but listening to
The murmur of the
Ebbing waters I shall
Weave my little web of
Dreams beneath the shadows
Cast by these dead iroko trees.

Of Poets, our Priests of Doubt

Shadow and Dream

a band of worshippers insolently intone
incantations beneath the tattered shawl of leaves

a little bird flaps its wings in the thin air
drenched in the full colour of sunset

a leaf stirs with the light wings of a meteor
and drops silently into my childhood nest of laughter

and I recall, through frayed amber edges of a blurred past
the memory of the strange quiet of an evening

an evening in the tale of elders
I recall a dream of wings and the horizon.

To all Compatriots

Brother,

I stretch out my hand
to reach for you in the dark
feeling for the warmth of love and life
and all I sense is the slippery touch of cobwebs

We are all in the dark
a dark cave from which despair threatens
we will braid these cobwebs
into tiny fingers of scars
and long threads of tears
a lacework of struggle and suffering

and then our laughter
 will roar on the rooftops!

Estrangement: Kano'78

(For a friend, Comrade Peasant)

Walking along craggy footpaths,
dusty, save for the lenience of the wind;
footpaths careering along a landscape
of drought, into the belly of a land
in famine

I watched

bare-footed children in ragged clothes,
white ragged clothes, (we are a
religious people), turning russet-coloured
in a silent covenant with the amber
of a waning day

I watched

shadows lengthening into the dusk,
the invasion of a gnawing silence,
shredded, occasionally, by animal sounds:
the whistle of a homing bird,
the frightened screech of an owl,
the hum of descending darkness
and

I went

passing on my way, herdsmen
returning, rod across the shoulders,
to the peasant peace of loving arms,
the pleasant filth of rotting shacks
but

I saw

the soothing pain of wounded dreams,
dreams shorn of wings, of colour,
of voice, of tone: dreams ruptured
in the rank screams of poli-trick-cians

In league

businessmen, professionals, prophets,
professors and
poets singing in the chloroform dream of money

And

I felt
I felt
estranged. Surely the poet is
estranged who cannot share
his people's fount of being.

Mind Buoys

(in a season of omens)

In the faint gleam of her eyes
Is the flicker of a dying dream
What flame will revive this dream?
What buoys to anchor a mind adrift?

I

The hawker of curses crowded with the cock
at sunrise
and we rose to a rain of tobacco-tainted
tubercular spitum
We will watch them, silently watch them
reap their garland of curses ...

II

We called a war without a cause
We found the cause in the battle
 When the blood of men tingled
in glasses of deceit ...

III

We sailed up a stream of sorrows
Seeking balms to soothe the sear
of sutured minds, oils to spread
on sprained souls ...

IV

But why, why do you flee from our

landscape of sorrows
come, come let us build here an altar
with the blood of our living martyrs ...

V

Sometimes, sometimes I wonder at the black hide
that shelters your throbbing blood
wonder at the almost inaudible tom-tom of your heart
and dream of the untold story that agitates your bosom ...

VI

Here our roads meet within the bean's eyebrow
here the sweat and tears of the years are hidden
Let us plant a seed on this earth a seed
that will flower on the face of the moon . .

VII

The wind has lent our song a sail
above their tear gas and their bullets
above their bloodlust and their fractured minds
the cannons of our laughter are strangely singing ...

VIII

If the wind is for us who can be against us?
We will watch the wine well on the lips of maidens
Smell the rain-fragrance of their songs and our
Exulted spirits will soar above the whirlwinds of hate ...

IX

A gleam of light touches lightly, moves, returns
Light on the first seed planted in earth

Look! this is a tendril seeking, seeking
The firm pillars of oak-minds ...

X

So reach out, reach out and clasp the rainbow
Between desire and the dream, the shadow and the tree
Reach out and clasp the sun and t!1e rain
Our shield against the seasons.

Dream: Sea, Moon, Bird

I

the sullen silent sea waiting
breathlessly
sourly panting from last wavelash

the gushing wave again wended its way
hurriedly
out of breath
with a slap and a dash
depositing its woe on shoreline
sea gulls, crabs, lobsters, fishes and all
dead with a breath on their eyes
about them a wreath of scars

II

lingering lustrous star
overhead
shyly
turns his head
and the old lady with a baby
on the crescent face of the moon squeaked

III

the egret with the beak of steel
has descended again below skyline
into our treasure-house of scars
cascading down on our scar-shrines
feigning maiden purity
she claws at our scars,
our only symbols of suffered ages ...

(The rain was soft that evening
and there was strength in the grove
where the Priest sat in habit, in dream,
reading the sacred kolanuts).

Scar Poem

(For Leroy Jones)

When they stopped him in his track
to ask for his scars, he said:
I am Cinna the Poet!
I am Cinna the Poet!
Poems are bullshit, yes bullshit
If you cannot show the scar
on the words. Bullshit!
Songs are bullshit, yes bullshit
If you cannot show the scar
in the voice. Bullshit!
So they murdered him before the sun
And poured the blood on their scars.

The Warrior's Love Song

Love Quartet

I

I sought you among these barren rocks
I sought your footprints in the sands
I sought your face among desert mirages
Among the clashing images of a decadent age

Like the wind in endless search I called
At waterless wells and dry fountains
Seeking the nest of your voice
Among the song-stores of estranged poets
And you came to me one blustery morning
When laughter exploded in the cheeks of children
And I saw your face in the rippling mirrors of the sea
You came to me with a grasshopper smell of fresh grass

The misty morning drips drowsy dew on your eyes
This dark-faced woman of my dream.

II

My Peasant Queen of Springs
You rose with the sun
Rinsed your eyelids with pure dewdrop
And threw off the enchanted veil of dawn

A smile is threading the thin spread of your lips
In white spitum—a smile beyond the lure of wine
Dancing patches of light filtered through palmfronds
Foretell our local lore of sunrise
And I who beheld your body naked as dawn
Before the stream with the scars of the past
Only I saw your unclad beauty

And felt your struggle against the sorrow of Seasons
Your beauty that never graced the backs of postcards
Your sorrow which could not bear the smear of print.

III

Miracle Woman, I'll sing your legend
In the homestead where hunger peers in the
face of toothless wisdom
In the streets where famished children longingly wait
Weary with hope for the blessing of rain

Miracle woman, I'll sing your legend
When the wind teases the leaves with wet dreams
When petals open expectant for rain
And granaries are filled beyond fruited dreams

The wind does not terrify the leaves
It only soothes the irritant eyelid itch
Your name is beyond the leer of robbers
And your peasant beauty beyond the curse of detractors

Miracle woman, I'll sing your legend
Till it kindles joy-kilns in the hearts of beggars.

IV

Listen to the murmur of these waves
 Riding the humps of the sea to these sands
The salty sigh of the tired mistresses of the sea
The white sweetness of the love in the coconut's heart
The mermaids were pulsating at the edge of the sea
Lending coral breath to the surf-washed pebbles
My voice was the thunder that scratched your doorstep
On a distant night seeking its fleeing echoes

That night when I slipped the wind of earth
Between your thighs in a joyous cascade of rain-flakes
When the seeds are dancing in the womb of the gourd
And the wine is fermenting in the gourd of your Womb
I'll await the birth of flowers on skeins of leaf
and this will be the moment of our love.

Communion

The wine we shared that night
Did not grow out of our heads
But out of the earth we trod
The wine we shared that night
Did not ferment in our souls
But out of the earth we trod
Between the kernel and the wine
In the ancient womb of earth
Has grown our brimful dream.

No songs tonight, my love

There are no songs, my love, no songs tonight
The moon has hidden its leprous face behind the trees
And the night threatens with darkness the last farmer's footfall

Evil birds are twitching, witches are wandering
And the owl with cold glassy eyes is hooting

There are no songs, my love, no songs tonight
The fire you see is not the lambent home hearth
Only the flame points of death seeking bullets
No songs my love: darkness and death, holding hands
Have come to steal the peace of sleep.

I want to dance out of my skin

out of your curious history
I take these phases of love and betrayal
I read them in fissures on my palm
They are braided into lines of anguish
in my stained memory.
(For Moremi)

You flushed the flurry of day
And the uncertain eagerness of night
With your moonlight presence

Like the wind you moved beneath the creepers
Exploring the secret of green leaves
Emerging, you lingered with your scars of love

Royal, your sadness is like a grain planted
In a night of blood, a night of love,
Your sadness is the betrayal of the Gods

Yet I want to dance in the blood
of your flesh, in the throbbing
pulse of your betrayed blood

In this time of betrayal of tribe and kin
I want to dance in your eyes of rain
Cleansed for the warrior's task
The rain is beating the rhythm of a leper's song
A god's kinsman is in a rage tonight
Hence

I can dance ecstatic before your presence
Like a tree on a windy day.
O! I want to dance out of my skin.

Songscars of Struggle

As you plaited the waves

(For the Aba Women Rioters)

I

As you plaited the waves
with your dainty maiden fingers
making nipples out of the wave-crests

I saw your scars swimming in the light ...

As you peeled off the banana coverings
throwing off the brasieres in ritual flips
floating like an eel into the waters

I saw your scars swimming in the light ...

As you dried your sandy delight in the sun
on the stream washed sands
weaving the sunlight into your soul

I saw your scars swimming in the light ...

Creaking on the hinges of your delight
I went with your fruits into the streets ...
Yesterday I saw you floating in the horizon of my face
Yesterday as your dewdrenched hair glistened
in the morning light
I made a flute from the bones of our dead
and on the banner of our land I painted you
a song of different colours
...out of the earth the thorns grow, out of our land ...

You were there at the wedding-feast
of earth and the birth of rain ...
As the wind carressed an altar-stone
in the lips of an ageless evening
You were there with your gift of light

... out of the earth the thorns grow, out of our land ...

From that grove O Poetess you took your being
out of the blood on the altar-stone
you forged your light of scars on the plinth of the wind

...out of the earth the thorns grow. out of our land ...

For this, for this alone
With my horn of scars
I lend your name forever to the seven winds.

Night

Dissolving in the interminable
echoes of your factory--
Night sandwiched between two days
with sounds echoing down uncertain ways--
I stand alone prying into Eshu's domain

Echoes of lost sounds
Reminisences of long forgotten dreams
Flap my dog ears with an unkind deliberation
Earth plant my being fast
Against the dissolution
of these sublime presences
Plant my spider legs into
The sockets of your new reality
And send me back into this
Cocoon of earthly harvest and comfort.

Bubble

Watching
a little bubble inflate itself
with the wind of a dream rising with the longing of hope
to fly from the depth of despair
to emerge from the quicksands of anguish
to stand daintily on a little tendril of love
to explode with the seminal fluid of sea-wine

I hold in my wounded breast the perpetual pain and its
memory
and hug with blood-warmth
the secret eternal pain and dream of a bubble.

Ashewo

The sun settles as usual
shattering red splinters about her.
The day winds up with the pungent smell
of incense in the wind's way.
{Cathedral incense and chimney smoke
combined to choke the stammering day
coughing out its lingering cobbles).

Set out as usual to watch
that violated goddess sit on her stool
asking with that legendary leer in her eyes
to be recognised, to be recognised,
seeking that spinner of yams to weave
her tale of woe.

Arrive today with a resolve, to say:
I know you-

though we do not speak in the same tongue,
I know your silence was fashioned in another's farm,
under the heat of the sun.
Now the sun is dying, slowly.
We will meet again at the great square
where our scars will be put on sale!

Arrive today with this resolve: and watch.

She will lift her watery gaze
from her limpid fingers
and spread her lonesome teeth
with a smile across the table.

Slave song or a flag

They led me in at the end of the tether
washed in coloured streams of light
They oiled all my scars
They oiled out all my sweat
And my body became one lucent mass

> *Let the word take root*
> *in the soil of our land*
> *Let the song take root*
> *it will grow into basketfulls of fruit*

They played me strange travesties of my native songs
In a hall teeming with echoes and shadows
They asked me to do a fertility dance
In a rite of impotence
They who had bled the sun for thirty moons
And castrated me and all my household
They asked me to do a fertility dance
In a rite of impotence

> *Let the sower plant his soul*
> *in this earth of our birth*
> *Let the sower plant his soul in earth*
> *it will grow into fruits of song*

I could not smell the greeness of earth
On the wake of rain or the coming of harvest
I could not see the light in the eyes of children
I could not see the roundness of the moon
Nor could I hear the gentle sizzle of rain
And the laughter of mothers
Yet they wanted me to do the dance or drifting pollens

Let the word take root
in the soil of our land
Let the song take root
it will grow into basketfulls of fruit

Yesterday when I saw buds in my eyes
And a green leaf sprouting from my forehead
I thought I was man again
O! I felt I was an orange tree
With phallic thorns that would pierce the wind
And rear the rainbow of love
Today I find it is all a flag

Let the sower plant his soul
in this earth of our birth
Let the sower plant his soul in earth
it will grow into fruits of song

Martyred May

May came trembling, hands and all
importunate as a lover's embrace

Your veins crawling in fiery skeins
Your fingers long and light
Sunburst of torchlike rays
Somnolent candle-flame-head fading into space
Oblong headed infinitude

I remember best your shy nervousness
Your spasmic breath as the blood rushed
Within ...

I can still hear across the distance
and the foil of time, my large booming voice
still across the rain of days
the nocturnal song of your voice as the moon
sallied with the time ...

All that is in the past now and memory
sun and the moon have woven more scars
into the fabric of day and night and the sea
is now dry leaving two shadowy scars of pain
a wilted water-lily and a coral.

Tower of dreams

let my hand touch yours
aross this mist of time:
a feel of the flesh
let my tear join yours
aross this gulf of anguish:
a well of water.
I will erect your suffering
into a tower of dreams for future generations.
(mother and child)

As she bent camel-burdened
With dawn bubbles between her teeth
Her human load crying on her back
She bunched up her buttocks and adjusted her hips
Again tying the new load with her ancient cloth
Waiting for the sun to rise above the rain at the cloud's end.

At suncall she will be here to reap
The delight of tears in the leaf's eye
For she has woven garlands of sorrow
On an eve that died with the wind's sigh
Among the twisted vines of unfulfilled dreams
She will be here to reap at suncall
The scar on the earth's skin, the memory
Of a wound that stirred its virgin flesh.

She will be here at sunrise a reaper of delight
Little buds of light on her breast her waist girdled
With green beads of vegetation.

Phoenix

(1949: Iva Valley, Enugu. For the murdered miners.)

He is a speck against the skyline,
a lone bird,
dawning,
draped in the blood of a rising sun,
out of the spent ashes of clouds,
out of the death of yesterday,
rending the transparent evil of veiled clouds
with the beak of love.

He is a lone bird,
full-fledged with memories,
dawning with the sun,
against this counterpane of ashen sky.

Prophecy

We will be here when it ends
Watching beyond clouds that
Have lost the will to gather

We will be here when it ends
Staring vacantly at cornices
Where evil eyes had been

We will be here when it all ends
When the harvest comes
On the fruit-fringes of rain

We will be here when it ends
Watching dancing silhouettes of skeletons
Drifting on a huge wave that leads to the desert.

Our Legacy

In the midst of my pain
I decked you in laughter-laurels
I left a song at your doorstep
When the wound festered in my breast

Though the wounds of that battle
We fought that children may share
In the grains of laughter have healed
The echoing scars of the past remain

I will forever cherish
Those pearls of laughter
And beads of song
For those are our only legacy.

Epitaph

Here is one who let his soul expand
With the wind of love
One who let his soul explode
With the fire of splitting pods
That seeds may scatter and take flesh
Within the fragile womb of dreams

Here is one who lives
At the beacon of time
He yeasted his blood with earth sod
That tears may cease
And fruits flourish on every farm
He lives in the bounty of harvest
And the fullness of song

His names are myriad

Kunle Adepeju
Akintunde Ojo
Soweto Stars etc.

Cherished crystals for the light of memory.

Home

Home:

and the whispers lull me on
0 that the cry of newborn babes
the laughter of women, sungleams in their eyes
the jives of drunken men, wine bubbles on their lips
welcome me.

Four Folk Figures

Cock

(for Walter Rodney)

a fluff of white feathers
idling by the crossroad criss-crossed
between night and day, the noon and the sun
you lingered waiting for the eye of the day

sleep-weary fluff of feathers
silent as a trembling leaf, winged with dewdrops
watching the fire-flies fade in the wake of dawn
you spread my dream on the tree's leaves

then suddenly
as you proclaimed the rise of the kingdom of the sun
from the long night of shadows that clouded our eyes
you saw a bowl of white-chalk at the crossroad
and from the hollow of the cowrie's eye
emerging from the jaws of the night came the lion
proclaiming the grave's grey dream of glut ...

Lion

(for the critic, Lionel!)

Slouching
out of the forest of dead leaves
with withered claws that hurt my nightsongs
and ravenous teeth that bit my song's finger of woe
he picked the cock clean of its flesh and feathers
 drinking in the fountain of its warm red blood
chewing at its red crest of the sun
and with a prize of fresh feathers tried to erase
the broken dream of its song, its crown of scars.

Snake

(at Lokoja, for Loretta)

a riddle on the bushpath of my life
under the blinding glare of the noonday sun
in this stillness where no leaves rustle
a snake, tongue/forked in a stinging smile,
tempts me with its glassy hypnotic eyes
and compels a choice between the beauty of the mirage
and the thorny tortuous road that leads homewards

absorbing its sting in my veins
I let the poison course through to my bitter roots
and I walk homewards on a marl-screen of mirages.

Tortoise

(for the Poet, Langston Hughes)

I have seen kingdoms,
traversed all the land
from the cockerel's dreamland
inhabited by the daughters of laughter
through the lion's flaming lair of blood
to the snake's tempting ecstacyworld of the flesh.
I have known them all, have known
that many rivers flow through all these lands
into the salty ocean of life
and have learnt without the beard of age,
to shelter it all within the shell of my life
for the spider has woven my broken shell
into a web of fantasy in which is container
the metaphoric lore of all my journeys.

A Bard and the Muse of Friendship

Harry Garuba's *Shadow and Dream* affirms his feat as a poet of many styles and many voices, one whose multitudinous themes are central to almost every important development in the postcolonial African state. His division of the collection into four parts: "Of Poets, our Priest of Doubt," "The Warrior's Love Song," "Songscars of Struggle," and "Four Folk Figures," that echo a truthful depiction of reality, a rejection of high art conventions, and a questioning of idealized beauty, makes him the Picasso of poetry, affirming his protean ability to be always a trailblazer of reform. And he himself alludes the poet's struggle with tradition, to the poet's constant need to search for a new system of expression when he refers to poets as "our Priests of Doubt". Garuba was, until his death, a poet perpetually in revolution against himself, against his own tradition, insisting that the word and song "take root in the soil of our land" and "grow into basketfuls of fruit" and "the sower plant his soul in this earth of our birth" and "it will grow into fruits of song" ("Slave song or a flag" 35). Perhaps for this reason he frequently had no difficulties in finding an initial acceptance for his poetry and consequently they are being republished posthumously.

Like most postcolonial African poetry, Garuba's *Shadow and Dream* will stimulate many to write about it and him, and for diverse reasons. There are many critics who would esteem the lyrical and metaphysical qualities of the work, some would find fault with its social commitment; others, sympathetic with the author's political concerns, would exalt the more militant aspects of his writing; and yet others would prefer to eschew politics almost entirely in their criticism, by studying the treatment accorded certain grand themes, like love ("No songs tonight, my love") and prostitution ("Ashewo"). The imminence of such a divergence of critical perspectives is perhaps to be expected, given the sumptuousness and multifariousness of Garuba's work. But one of the things that this republication seeks, I believe, is an integrative view, a nonpartisan reassessment of *Shadow and Dream*'s the political and the nonpolitical, so as to determine its uniqueness in the larger context of Garuba's other works and postcolonial African poetry. For this reason, in this epilogue, I have neither contended a thesis, nor have I tried to explain all the poems in *Shadow and Dream*, which would be a monumental task. My intention is more modest: to suggest the groundwork for agreement on the literary significance of Garuba's poetry. Regular readers of Garuba's works would find a wealth of new insights and analyses each time they (re)read *Shadow and Dream* as it brilliantly (re)considers current controversies in postcolonial African socioeconomics and politico-culture. A hugely provocative, far-reaching, comprehensive and accessible collection for scholars engaged across disciplines, *Shadow and Dream* challenges and rewards the reader through its significant contributions to the roots and routes it offers to the construction of postcolonial African futures.

Even though as a student of African literature I had unavoidably introduced myself to Garauba's work through the internet, I first met him in 2019 when he and his friend and colleague, Professor Francis Nyamnjoh, visited the University of Ghana, Legon, where I was pursuing a postdoc fellowship. At that time in my life, I was hungry for stories about the works and lives of prominent African writers and critics. I was figuring out who I was, and how my academic experiences, largely Cameroonian/African and relatively underprivileged, measured up. Where did I stand, and what was my responsibility to students of African literature? The brief conversation I had with Garuba buttressed my conviction that there was something I had to do: I had to listen to people like him and above all, I had to be willing to see what they had written/were writing. We made plans about mentoring and kept communication vibrant especially as I was excitedly battering him with emails and WhatsApp texts. Even while at the hospital Professor Garuba painstakingly encouraged me to apply for a postdoc fellowship at the Centre for African Studies (CAS), University of Cape Town. Thanks to his heartbreaking generosity, I would later get a postdoc on "Entanglements, Mobility and Improvisation: Culture and Arts in Contemporary African Urbanism and its Hinterlands" and would eventually be associated with UCT for 2 years. I spent the last two months of my postdoc in Ghana devouring Garuba's challenging creative and intimidating critical works. On February 3, 2020, I moved back to Cameroon and on the morning of the 28th of the same month, both Garuba and my father passed on as if they had conspired to orphanize me. Each time I ask myself: why them? I never find the answer, as though not knowing is a condition for love. Maybe the understanding of the heart requires no words, needs no language but it is such love that inspires me and keeps blossoming when I am afforded the opportunity to say something about Garuba's works.

Hassan M. Yosimbom
Postdoc Fellow
(January 2021 – December 2022)
University of Cape Town

Printed in the United States
by Baker & Taylor Publisher Services